Newcastle's Old Pubs

by Andrew Clark

The Stack Hotel and the trolley bus terminus on Church Street, Walker, around 1936. Trolley buses ran in Newcastle from the mid 1930s to the mid 1960s. The Stack Hotel survived a little longer, until the early 1970s. There is an earlier view of the Stack Hotel on page 11.

Previous page: The Lord Hill on the corner of Pitt Street and Barrack Road in the early 1900s. The pub was one of a number owned by Richard Charlton. A sign on the pub says 'Supplied direct from Charltons' Bonds' which was the company's warehouse, bottling factory and offices in nearby Waterloo Street. A 1960s view of the pub can be seen on page 15.

Copyright Andrew Clark 2015

First published in 2015 by

Summerhill Books
PO Box 1210, Newcastle-upon-Tyne NE99 4AH

www.summerhillbooks.co.uk

email: summerhillbooks@yahoo.co.uk

ISBN: 978-1-906721-92-3

Contents

Two old pubs that are still very popular today – the Free Trade Inn (*above left*) in St Lawrence Road and the Trent House (*above right*) in Leazes Lane.

The Northumberland Arms on Northumberland Street. This was one of a number of pubs that were demolished in the 1970s to make way for new developments in Newcastle. The area around the Northumberland Arms was replaced with the Eldon Square shopping centre.

Acknowledgements

Summerhill Books would like to thank the following people who have helped in the publication of this book: D. Allan, Alan Brett, Philip Curtis, John Davison, George Nairn, Sharyn Taylor, Mike Young, Yvonne Young, Beamish Museum, West Newcastle Picture History Collection.

We would also like to acknowledge the following breweries and wine & spirit merchants: Scottish & Newcastle, Vaux, James Deuchar, Robert Deuchar, W.B. Reid, Greenalls, Watneys, Richard Charlton, James Robinson & Sons, Swinburne & Co, Stokoe & Co.

Summerhill Books

Summerhill Books publishes North East local history books.

To receive a catalogue of our titles, send a stamped addressed envelope to:

Andrew Clark, Summerhill Books, PO Box 1210, Newcastle-upon-Tyne NE99 4AH

or email: summerhillbooks@yahoo.co.uk

or visit our website to view our full range of books: **www.summerhillbooks.co.uk**

Introduction

This is not a complete history of the public houses of Newcastle but a glimpse into the rich heritage of the licensing and brewing trade of Tyneside from the mid 19th century to present day. That history is told through old pictures, postcards, drawings, adverts and modern day photographs. Alongside these illustrations are many old 'pub tales'.

Pubs are a fascinating subject for local history and an interesting way to look at how Newcastle has changed over the years. The story of the changes in the city's housing, work, sport, entertainment can be told through the history of local pubs. For example, Scotswood Road was known for its numerous pubs and alongside these were local shops, factories and people's homes. Today, Scotswood Road is very different – the pubs and houses have gone and instead other businesses have moved in, replacing the heavy industry that once dominated the area.

Many of these social changes can be seen through the history of public houses – an ideal way to celebrate our area's heritage.

The Old George Inn – Newcastle's oldest pub. Situated in Old George Yard, off High Bridge, the inn dates from the late 1500s and is still going strong today.

Along the way we'll see the rise and fall of the local brewers and remember some of the brands of beer – some well known while others have almost been forgotten. Sporting links with pubs are featured as well as stories of coaching inns, grand hotels, the Temperance movement and even old songs.

Throughout the book there are 'pub tales' which tell stories of individual pubs, landlords and customers.

I hope you enjoy the book and if you have any information on the old pubs of Newcastle or any 'pub tales', please contact me.

Andrew Clark
Summerhill Books
March 2015

Right: The Boat House Inn on Scotswood Road – one of many pubs on a road that was known for 'a pub on every corner'. This public house, like many in this book, has now gone. More old pubs on Scotswood Road are featured on page 22.

The Beer is fine at the Blue Star Sign

An advert for Newcastle Breweries from 1938 with the slogan: 'the beer is fine at the Blue Star sign'. First introduced by the brewery in the 1920s, the Blue Star became a recognised symbol for pubs and beer in Newcastle and throughout the North East.

The Blue Star hangs from the White Horse in the Groat Market. The pub was demolished in the 1960s and Thomson House (home of the Chronicle and Journal) built on the site.

Two Blue Star pubs in the 1970s. *Above left*: The Railway Hotel, Benfield Road, Walker that, in 2015, still has the Blue Star on the building. *Above right*: The Brandling Villa on Haddricks Mill Road, Gosforth. Both pubs are still open in 2015.

Other former Blue Star pubs featured in this book are: the Free Trade Inn, St Lawrence Road (page 3); the Trent House, Leazes Lane (page 3); the Colliery Engine Inn, Shields Road (page 11); the Black Bull, Barrack Road (page 14); the Robin Adair, Scotswood Road (page 24); the Grace Inn and the Heaton Hotel, Shields Road (page 32); the Whin Dyke, Denton Park (page 38) and the Bay Horse, Westgate Road (page 41).

THE TYNE BREWERY, NEWCASTLE UPON TYNE
Home of Newcastle Blue Star Beers

A trade card produced by Scottish & Newcastle with the old 1884 brewery superimposed on to an aerial view when the company dominated this part of the city in the 1960s. St James' Park can just be seen in the top right hand corner. While the football ground has been rebuilt and is now one of the best stadiums in the country, the brewery site has been cleared. Today, Newcastle University Business School, Science Central, a hotel, a restaurant, shops and student accommodation occupy the area.

Newcastle Breweries was formed in 1890 when five local companies merged. One of these firms was John Barras & Co and it is their 1884 Brewery that can be seen above. John Barras was originally a Gateshead company who bought their first premises there in 1770.

The late 19th and early 20th centuries saw massive expansion for the brewer and in 1927 its most famous beer was first produced – Newcastle Brown Ale.

After the Second World War, Newcastle Breweries continued to grow. They acquired hundreds of pubs and took over a number of breweries and wine & spirit merchants – including James Deuchar (see page 26) and Robert Deuchar (see page 27). In 1960 a merger took place with Scottish Breweries to form Scottish & Newcastle. The company thrived for a further 45 years before the closure of the Tyne Brewery in 2005.

Right: All that is left from the old Tyne Brewery is this carved date stone that stands on the redeveloped site in Blue Star Square. 'Established A.D. 1770' refers to John Barras' company and 'removed from Gateshead 1884' is the date when that brewer moved to Newcastle.

19th Century Landlords and Pubs

Below is a song, by William Watson, celebrating Newcastle landlords from the 19th century – originally published in *Allan's Tyneside Songs* (1891).

Chorus
Then hey for good drinking,
It keeps us from thinking,
We all love a drop in our turn.

Kind friends and acquaintance, attention I claim,
While a few jolly landlords in this town I name;
In alphabet order my song it is penn'd,
And I hope, for joke's sake, it will never offend.

A stands for Armfield, a good hearty blade,
Tho' he's left the Nag's Head, still follows his trade;
At the foot of the Market you'll find his new shop,
Where many an old friend still calls in for a drop.

B stands for Burns, of the Theatre Square;
She's an orderly woman – good drink is sold there;
If I wanted a wife, I should readily choose,
This amiable widow to govern my house.

C stands for Cant, sign of the Blue Bell,
Who keeps a good house, and good porter doth sell;
Quarrelling or fighting, is there seldom seen,
She's a canny old widow, but rather too keen.

D for Dixon, who once kept the Unicorn-Ho!
And D Stands, for Dixon, White Hart, you well know;
Then there's Dixon, Quayside, just a little way down –
Were the three fattest landlords in all the whole town.

E stands for Eggleton, Fighting Cocks Inn,
Tho' old took a young wife, and thought it no sin;
F for Finlay, his shop's corner of Pudding Chare,
And good wine and spirits you'll always get there.

The 'Cross Room' in the White Hart Inn, 1845.

The Scotch Inn, Bigg Market in the 17th century. It later became the Fighting Cocks Inn.

The notorious Hell's Kitchen in the Flying Horse, the Groat Market. It was well known in the early part of the 19th century as a gathering place for 'eccentric characters of Newcastle'. On the right, with the fiddle, is 'Blind Willie'.

G is for Gibson, the Blue Posts, in Pilgrim Street,
Where a few jolly souls oft for harmony meet;
H for Hackworth in Cowgate, Grey Bill is the sign
Only taste his good ale-faith, you'll say its divine.

H stands for Heron, the sign of the Cock;
H for Hall, near Nuns' Gate keeps a snug oyster shop;
H stands for Horn, and he's done very weal,
Since he bother'd the heart of sly Mrs Neil.

I stands for Inns – we've the best in the North,
There's the King's Head, the Queen's Head,
    the George and the Turf;
The Old Crown and Thistle, and Miller's Half Moon,
Well known to the Trav'lers who frequent the town.

K stands for Kitchen, Hell's Kitchen 'Twas nam'd,
And long for good ale and good spree has been fam'd;
In each parlour, in vestry, or kitchen you'll find,
The beer drawer, Mary, obliging and kind.

L stands for Larkin – he's left the Black Boy,
Once fam'd for Patlanders and true Irish joy;
On the Scotswood New Road a house he has ta'en,
Where I hope the old soul will get forward again.

M stands for Mitford – he kept the North Pole,
Just over Leazes, a dull looking hole;
Now our favourite poet lives at Head on the Side,
Here's success to his muse – long may she preside.

N stands for Newton, sign of the Dolphin,
Who the old house pull'd down, built it up like an inn;
They say he found gold – how much I can't tell,
But never mind that, he's done wonderful well.

O stands for Orton – he keeps the Burnt House,
Once fam'd for the knights of the thimble and goose;
And O Stands for Ormston at Pandon O rare!
Temptation enough for young men that go there.

P stands for Pace, sign of White Swan,
Who, for to oblige, will do all that he can;
A convenient house, when you marketing make,
To pop in and indulge yourself with a beefsteak.

R stands for Ridley and Reed, you all know,
And R stands for Richardson – all in a row;
First, Three Tuns, the Sun, and the Old Rose and Crown,
And their ale's good as any at that part of the town.

S for Sayers, Nag's Head – he keeps good mountain dew;
Only Taste it, You'll find what I tell you is true,
S for Stokoe, wine merchant, foot of St John's Lane;
For good stuff and good measure we'll never complain.

T for Teasdale, the Phoenix – a house fam'd for flip;
T for Teasdale, who once kept the sign of the Ship;
And W for Wylam, a place more fam'd still;
Sure you all know the Custom House on the Sandhill.

The Grey Horse Tavern on the Quayside. Mentioned in the line: 'Black, White, and Grey Horse, and Flying Horse too.'

The Old Robin Hood Inn, Pilgrim Street, 1860. Ten years later the inn was one of a number in Newcastle raided by the police, as reported in the Newcastle Courant on 22nd July 1870:

'Adam Edmonds, landlord of the Robin Hood Inn, was charged with selling foreign wines without a licence. Isabella Welford, Dog Bank, Margaret Stephenson, Forth Banks, Joshua Greenwell, Oyster Shell Lane; Wm Gair, Stockbridge; and Joseph Westmoreland, Fighting Cocks Inn, Denton Chare, were charged with a similar offence ... an excise officer visited the house of each of the defendants and purchased a glass of port or sherry. They supplied him with foreign wines, for which they had no licence ... A fine of £5 was inflicted in each case.'

Robin Hood, Dog and Cannon, and Tiger for me,
The Peacock, well known to the clerks on the Quay;
The Old Beggar's Opera for stowrie, my pet,
Mrs Richardson's was – and she cannot be bet.

There's the Black Bull, and Grey Bull, well known to a few;
Black, White, and Grey Horse, and Flying Horse too.
The Black House, the White House, the Hole in the Wall,
And the Seven Stars, Pandon, if you dare to call.

There's the Turk's Head, Nag's Head and Old Barley Mow,
The Bay Horse, the Pack Horse and Teasdale's Dun Cow;
The Ship and the Reel, the Half Moon and the Sun;
But I think, my friends, it is time to be done.

Then, each landlord and lady, wish them success,
Town and trade of the Tyne, too – we cannot do less;
And let this be the toast when we meet to regale
'May we ne'er want a bumper of Newcastle ale'.

Pubs for the Workers

Right: An advert from Newcastle Breweries from 1948 that was aimed at a furnaceman – 'After a good day's work for Britain – that's when beer is best'. This was one in a series of adverts by the brewery that targeted different trades. At this time heavy industry and drinking (sometimes heavy as well) went hand-in-hand for some.

To the furnaceman good beer is an essential accompaniment to his day's work. Afterwards, it provides the relaxation that enables him to restore his energy for the new day ahead.

After a good day's work for Britain—that's when **beer is best**

BLUE STAR ALES are on sale in the buffet.

THE NEWCASTLE BREWERIES LTD.

Two pubs on Scotswood Road with names linked to the nearby Armstrong Works – The Forge Hammer Inn (*above*) and the Hydraulic Crane – for a time called Armstrong's Hydraulic Crane (*right*).

W.G. Armstrong built his factory at Elswick in the mid 19th century to manufacture cranes and hydraulic equipment. Employing thousands of local people, Armstrong was one of the most successful businessmen in the country and later became Lord Armstrong. Armaments were also manufactured and again local pubs such as the Rifle (see page 22) and the Gun took their name from this industry.

Armstrong's merged with Whitworth and then with Vickers in 1927. Vickers-Armstrong manufactured armaments, ships, aircraft and military vehicles.

Left: Workers leaving the Armstrong Works in the early 1900s. How many of these were off for a pint in one of the several pubs that were opposite the works?

Right: The Stack Hotel on Church Street, Walker, had plenty of miners for customers, being so close to the Jane Pit whose pulley wheel can be seen in the background.

Evan Martin, a local historian and whose father was a miner, said pitman needed to drink: 'Men at the pit worked hard and got dust on their chests and so they drank. I knew men who as soon as they finished work and got bathed, went to the pub or club. But there was very little binge drinking like there is today.'

There were a number of pubs in Newcastle that had names connected with mining, such as the Colliery Engine Inn on Shields Road, Walker (*right*), the Coal Wagon (Walker) and the Miners' Arms (Scotswood Road).

Left: A smiling miner from a National Coal Board advert.

Shipyard workers liked a pint as well and here is the Neptune Hotel that was next to the Neptune Yard of Swan Hunter's, Walker. Visitors to the yard often stayed overnight at the hotel.

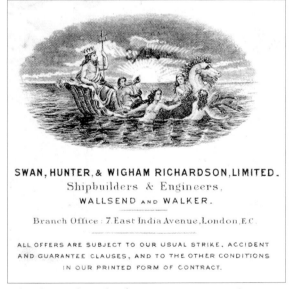

The letterhead of Swan, Hunter & Wigham Richardson Limited – shipbuilders and engineers of Wallsend and Walker.

Bill Purdie started work at Swan Hunter's in the 1930s and recalls the men at work in the yard and then in the pub: 'Foremen wore three piece suits, skilled men wore boilersuits, engineers and fitters wore blue, and carpenters, shipwrights, platers and cranedrivers wore brown bib and brace overalls with a jacket of the same material … This distinction was applied in the pubs as well. Foremen, having replaced their obligatory and distinctive bowler hats for cloth caps or trilby hats, invariably inhabited the 'snug' whilst the skilled and unskilled men used the bar.'

Then & Now

Pubs are constantly changing. Sometimes the exterior gets a make over while often the interior is redesigned when fashion or the use of the pub changed. In the 1960s and '70s, traditional pubs were seen as old fashioned and the 'new age' brought in the latest designs and name changes. Some pubs with several small rooms had them knocked into one large space and then given a trendy name to attract the 'young crowd'.

Today, many of these fashions have come full circle and pubs try to go back to a more traditional style and an old name – often at great expense.

Above: The Victoria & Comet Hotel in Neville Street around 1960. In the fifty-five years since this photograph was taken, this pub opposite the Central Station has gone through a number of name changes. It was a Yates's Wine Lodge in the 1970s and then in the 1990s it joined the trend of Irish names, being called first Durty Nelly's and then O'Neil's.

In 2015 (*below*) the pub is now called the Victoria Comet so almost reverting back to its original name. As can be seen in the photograph below, the ground floor exterior is black – a common feature on a number of city centre pubs today.

Left: Two views of the Percy Arms in Percy Street. The top left photograph dates from after 1939 when it was bought by Vaux and alterations made. Like a number of Vaux pubs, it has that distinctive tiled band around the building (see the Tanners Arms opposite). This has disappeared in the 2015 photo bottom left. The weather vane on top of the pub has survived a hundred years of make-overs and changes in ownership.

One of the few survivors of the many pubs just off Scotswood Road is the Globe in Railway Street (*seen above left in the 1930s*). Today the Globe is a popular music venue (*above right*).

A familiar landmark as you approach Byker Bridge is the Tanners Arms (*above left with its tiled frontage*). Once a Vaux house, today its exterior, like a lot of modern pubs, now advertises food as well as alcohol (*above right*).

Right: The Queen Victoria Hotel, Gosforth, in 1956 in the last days under the sign of James Deuchar's Lochside Ales. Newcastle Breweries acquired the Scottish brewery owned by Deuchar's in this year.

Right: The Queen Victoria in 2015. The pub stands on a busy corner of Gosforth High Street and Salters Road. Even sixty years ago, traffic must have been a problem in this area as the photograph above includes a set of traffic lights – not that common in 1956 when there was a lot less cars on the road.

The Black Bull, Barrack Road, in the early 1900s. Tram lines turn the corner from Barrack Road into Stanhope Street with children standing in the road in their bare feet. The name above the door is 'G. McConachie'.

A redeveloped Black Bull, fifty to sixty years after the photograph above. The terraced houses on either side of the pub have gone and have been replaced by blocks of flats in the background. There are no tram lines but the overhead electric lines for the trolley buses remain.

The Black Bull in 2015. Both the pub and the flats behind show signs of improvements. This busy corner of Barrack Road and Stanhope Street now needs a set of lights to control the traffic. In the foreground there are fences, signs, road markings and other 'street furniture' making it a much more crowded scene compared with the two earlier photographs.

Sporting Connections – Football

Public houses played an important part in the early history of football in Newcastle. In the 1880s and 1890s, the two prominent local clubs were Newcastle East End and Newcastle West End.

West End, after playing at a couple of venues, eventually settled at St James' Park. In the early days the players changed at the nearby Lord Hill public house on Barrack Road (*seen on the right in the 1960s*). The licensee of the pub, John Black, was one of the backers of West End and later a director of Newcastle United.

In 1890, Newcastle East End issued a share offer and a number of people who invested in the club were from the pub trade. These included the brewer Robert Deuchar and his son Farquhar as well as the licensees of the Gosforth Hotel, the Chester (Shieldfield), the Glendale (Byker) and the Northumberland Arms.

The two rival teams eventually merged in 1892 to become Newcastle United, playing at St James' Park. The club and its players continued to have strong links with pubs and the brewing industry for the next 100 years.

The Lord Hill was demolished in the 1960s and replaced with The Magpie club (*below*). Student accommodation now stands on this area near to St James' Park.

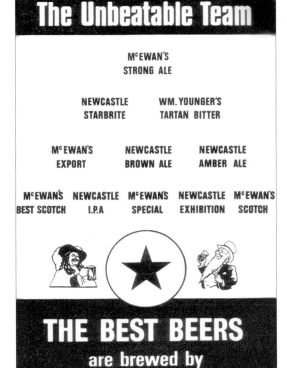

The 1980-81 season saw the start of shirt sponsorship on the famous black and white strips when a deal was agreed with Scottish & Newcastle Breweries for £100,000. Six years later, the Lancashire brewer Greenalls became sponsors only for Scottish & Newcastle to return during Kevin Keegan's time as manager. In the 1990s, brands such as McEwan's Lager and Newcastle Brown Ale appeared on shirts.

Left: This advert from Scottish & Newcastle shows how football has been used to promote alcohol for years. It was originally printed in a football programme in 1969 and shows 11 'best beers' lined up in an attacking 2−3−5 formation.

Right: An unusual illustration of Newcastle United goalkeeper Albert McInroy. The England international was signed from Sunderland in 1929 and played in the United team that won the 1932 FA Cup by beating Arsenal at Wembley. After retiring from football he followed the profession of a number of players – he became a publican. After a spell at the Bacchus in Newgate Street,

A. McINROY

Albert moved to the Havelock Arms, Newbottle, near Houghton-le-Spring and was landlord there for over 25 years. *Above right*: Albert McInroy behind the bar of the Havelock Arms.

Above: The Cradlewell on Jesmond Road where Bobby Mitchell (*above right*) was landlord in the 1970s. Mitchell, known as 'Bobby Dazzler', was one of Newcastle United's great players in the 1950s and helped the club win three FA Cups. Despite this success he did not enjoy the financial rewards that footballers do today. Mitchell played during the era of the 'maximum wage' which lasted until 1961 when it was £20 a week. When it was abolished the top players' wages jumped by almost five times that amount. Although footballers were still better paid than the average worker they were never given the rewards that today's stars receive and so Mitchell and his team-mates would need to find a new career when their playing days were over. As well as being at the Cradlewell, Bobby was also landlord at the Lochside in Heaton (see page 26).

Right: A Newcastle Breweries' advert congratulating Newcastle on winning the FA Cup for the second time in a row in 1952. The Cup was won for a third time in five years in 1955 with Bobby Mitchell scoring one of the goals in a 3-1 victory against Manchester City.

Champions again!

THE NEWCASTLE BREWERIES LTD.

Right: Newcastle legend, Kevin Keegan, on a Newcastle Breweries' beer mat advertising 'Blue Star Soccerdays' for children. Unlike former United players, McInroy and Mitchell, Keegan was very well paid during his playing career. After making his name at Liverpool, the England forward moved for a record fee to Hamburg and then later to Southampton. The football world was rocked when one of the biggest names of the 1970s and early '80s, and former European Footballer of the Year, signed for Newcastle United in 1982. Keegan was then on the massive wage of £3,000 a week and Scottish & Newcastle Breweries contributed towards his salary. His two seasons for the Magpies were worth the money as he helped secure promotion to the First Division. During this time he often made personal appearances to promote Scottish & Newcastle.

Ten years later Keegan returned to St James' as manager and a new golden era for the club began. He again led the club to promotion before creating an entertaining side that almost won the Premier League in 1996.

Above: The Strawberry, in the shadow of St James' Park, is a favourite pub for a pint before and after the match.

Since the formation of the Premier League in 1992 and live games being broadcast on television, the pub has been a popular place to watch football. During the 2014 World Cup it was estimated that each game was worth over £20 million of revenue to Britain's pub trade.

Right: One of many adverts that use football to sell beer – this time Watneys Red Barrel which was very popular in the 1960s and '70s. The brewer sponsored the Watney Cup in the early 1970s. This competition was played before the start of the football season between four teams who were the leading scorers in each division and who had not won promotion or qualified for Europe.

Full time

Half time

Time for another

RED BARREL-
WATNEYS KEG

Trust it—it's always clear, always in perfect condition

Also: WATNEYS PALE ALE · WATNEYS BROWN ALE
MANNS AND CREAM LABEL STOUT

Coaching Inns and Charabancs

In the days before the railway, the main form of travelling from one end of the country to the other was by horse-drawn coach. One of the main stops for coaches in Newcastle was the Turf Hotel in Collingwood Street. The following account from the *Monthly Chronicle of North Country Lore and Legend* (1888) describes the 'palmy days of Newcastle coaching':

'The term 'hotel' was used to indicate that sleeping accommodation was provided for travellers, in contradistinction to inns or taverns. The fame of the Turf soon became known to all who had to travel between north and south. There was no night coach except the 'Mail'; those, therefore, who came up by the day coach from Edinburgh had perforce to stay for the night in Newcastle, and proceed, say, at 6 or 8 o'clock next morning to London by the 'Wellington' or 'Highflyer,' travelling all night, the former reaching the Bull and Mouth, Aldersgate Street, about 4 pm, and the 'Highflyer' the White Horse, Fetter Lane, London, about 6 pm the following day.

The London to Edinburgh coach outside the Turf Hotel, Collingwood Street.

'Passengers who came from London, York or Leeds in like manner halted at the Turf Hotel, and went north by the 'Union' at 6 am, by Alnwick and Berwick to Edinburgh or by the 'Wellington' at 7 am by Wooler, Coldstream, Kelso, & c, each arriving between 8 and 9 the same evening at the Black Bull Inn, situate at the top of Leith Walk, Edinburgh.

'Another coach was afterwards started called the 'Express' and this left for York at the more convenient hour of 10 am, the passengers sleeping at York, going on to London about 9 the next morning, and arriving about the same hour the following day at the Saracen's Head, Snow Hill, London …

The Turf Hotel in 1888 after the days of the horse-drawn coach. The hotel survived until the late 19th century

'In the palmy days of Newcastle coaching – from about 1825 to 1834 one of the sights of Newcastle was the fine array of coaches opposite the Turf Hotel in an afternoon to be ready for the next morning. The horses were in teams, grey, black and bay. The Turf Hotel continued to afford accommodation for guests who found it necessary to stay overnight, until 1847, when the York and North Midland Railway to Newcastle was opened. The coaches to the south soon ceased to run, but those to Edinburgh were continued for some time longer. All the famous old inns on the Great North Road were closed one after another until none was left. Of course the Turf Hotel suffered, but it had a good name, and managed to survive the loss of custom through the advent of the iron horse.'

Above: A charabanc trip outside the Pine Apple Inn around 1913. Outings such as these would have been a real highlight either side of the First World War. Holidays were almost unknown for most people and day trips on charabancs would be as far as anyone would go. This is an all-male group and perhaps they were off for a day at the races or a visit to the countryside or seaside. The pub was in Pine Street, Elswick and closed after the First World War.

Above: Two adverts from the 1930s encouraging cyclists and walkers to call into Blue Star pubs for 'a timely pause' or 'wayside halt'.

Just before the Second World War, walking and cycling holidays or day trips were very popular when only a few people had cars. And for those who could afford a few nights away, a room at a pub such as the Newcastle House Hotel in Morpeth (*left*) would have been ideal.

Pub Tales

The Scottish Giant

William Campbell (*left*) was the manager of the Duke of Wellington, also known as Stokoe's, in High Bridge. Born in Glasgow in 1856, it was said that he weighed 52 stones when he died at the pub aged only 22 years. He must have been an imposing figure behind the bar as he was six foot four inches in height with 96 inch shoulders and a 76 inch chest!

Right: The Duke of Wellington in High Bridge, 2015. The premises were once owned by Stokoe & Co Wine Merchants.

Lamberts Leap

The Lamberts Leap was on Sandyford Road and is seen here on the right in the 1960s – with a scooter, typical of the period, outside. The unusual name comes from an incident in 1759 when a young man survived a miraculous fall. Cuthbert Lambert was riding his horse on Sandyford Lane when he approached a bridge over a deep dene. For some unknown reason the horse bolted and the rider was unable to stop the mare galloping towards the bridge and jumping over the side. They fell over 30 feet to the bottom of the dene.

Fortunately, the branch of a tree helped to break his fall and Lambert survived. Sadly the horse died. Lambert's lucky escape became a local legend and many years later gave its name to the pub not far from the 'leap'. This Robert Deuchar pub was demolished in the early 1970s.

The Little Waster

Left: An advert for Lorimers Best Scotch featuring one of the great North East comedians – Bobby Thompson. Known as the 'Little Waster', his career started in the 1950s but it was in the 1970s that he achieved his greatest success. Dressed in his trademark jumper and flat cap, Bobby toured the region's clubs with an act based mainly on stories of debt. Another part of his act was memories of the war and he is seen dressed in uniform in the Lorimers advert – and wearing the famous jumper on the far left.

The Pub Under the Bridge

Right: The Newcastle Arms (now called the Bridge Tavern) on Akenside Hill stands in the shadow of the Tyne Bridge. Originally, a 19th century tavern, it was rebuilt in the 1920s during the construction of the bridge and supports for the famous Tyneside landmark can be seen either side of the pub.

Below: The Tyne Bridge during construction in January 1928. By October of that year, it would be complete and opened by George V.

The New Tyne Bridge. (11th January) 1928. 29

A Postcard from the Past

Today, most people rarely send postcards but for the first half of the 20th century they were an important form of communication. In the days before telephones, email or texts, the postcard was often the quickest way to send a message.

On the right is the back of a trade card for John R. Hudspith, Ale and Porter Stores, from around 1915. Customers would fill in the card with their order of Whitbread Stout, Pale Ale etc and return it to Hudspith's Bell Terrace office (using a $^1/_2$d stamp). At this time there would have been

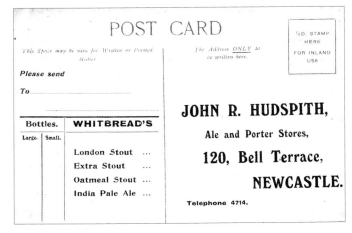

several deliveries of post a day so a card posted on a morning would normally arrive by that afternoon. Not as quick as a text or email but not bad for a hundred years ago.

Scotswood Road
A Pub on Every Corner

Ward's Trade Directory of 1911-12 listed the following pubs on Scotswood Road:

Pub	Number
Hydraulic Crane	903
Elswick Hotel	876
Gun Hotel	818
Crooked Billet	734
Vulcan Inn	640
Dene Hotel	630
Rifle Hotel	543
Ordnance Arms	467
Flax Mill Hotel	427
Freemasons' Arms	420
Park Road Hotel	404
Falcon Inn	336
Bath Hotel	305
Green Tree	266
Royal Oak	222
Shipwrights' Arms	203
Maid of Derwent	174
Duke of Cumberland	157
Lord Wharncliffe	146
Fountain Inn	126
Elswick House	110
Farmers Inn	98
Blenheim Hotel	96
Marlborough	78
Golden Eagle	42
King's Head	2

Listed at the Borough Boundary:

Ord Arms

Delaval Arms

The list above is only a fraction of the pubs that used to be on Scotswood Road. Others that many will remember include: the Boat House Inn, the Grapes, Clasper Arms, Moulders Arms and Mechanics Arms.

Three 'corner' pubs on the south side of Scotswood Road were: Bath Hotel (*above*), Flax Mill Hotel (*below*) and the Rifle Hotel (*bottom*). They were all listed in the directory of 1911-12 but were gone by the 1960s.

Above: Customers gathered outside the Dene Hotel on Scotswood Road around 1900. A number of signs say 'Supplied by Swinburne & Co' who were a Gateshead company and one of several local brewers and wine & spirit merchants who merged in 1890 to form Newcastle Breweries. The Dene Hotel, on the corner of Georges Road, closed in the early 1970s.

Right: The Royal Oak, a Scotswood Road pub that was also on the corner of Ivy Street and Oak Street. An advert for Lochside Ales can be seen on the left.

The Maid of Derwent on the corner of Maple Street and Scotswood Road.

The Blenheim Hotel – another Scotswood Road pub that closed in the 1960s.

'Gannin' along the Scotswood Road to see the Blaydon Races'

An advert for John Balmbra's Wheat Sheaf Inn, Cloth Market. It was here in 1862 that Geordie Ridley first performed the Tyneside anthem – 'Blaydon Races'.

Aw went to Blaydon Races,
'twas on the ninth of joon,
Eiteen hundred and' sixty-two,
On a summer's afternoon;

Aw tyuk the 'bus frae Balmbra's,
An' she wis heavy laden,
Away we went alang Collingwood Street,
That's on the road to Blaydon.

One of the pubs that once stood on Scotswood Road is mentioned in a line in the song:

We flew past Armstrong's factory;
And up to the Robin Adair,
Just gannin' doon te the railway bridge,
The bus wheel flew off there

The lasses lost their crinolines off,
An' the veils that hide their faces,
An' aw got two black eyes an' a
Broken nose in gan te Blaydon Races.

In 1962 a parade took place to celebrate the 100th anniversary of Geordie Ridley's song and here an omnibus makes its way to Scotswood Bridge. There were also floats of local companies, marching bands, servicemen and a centenary queen in her own carriage. Crowds lined the route that started from Balmbra's in the city centre, then along Scotswood Road to Blaydon.

Above: The Robin Adair – not the pub mentioned in 'Blaydon Races' but a 1960s version. The Robin Adair was built to replace the Ord Arms (*left*) in 1965 and was named after an older pub that had once stood on Scotswood Road. On the right hand side of the pub can be seen a mural of a horse-drawn carriage from the time of the Blaydon Races.

Left: Bridge Crescent with the Ord Arms in the background in the early 1900s. When the pub was demolished in the 1960s, the clock tower was moved to the Tyne Brewery. The Ord Arms' replacement – the Robin Adair – was itself closed and demolished in the 1990s.

Beer & Brewers

Brown Ale

Right: Newcastle Brown Ale being advertised in 1962 as 'now available in cans'.

This iconic beer became one of the North East's greatest exports after it was first launched in 1927 – although since the closure of the Tyne Brewery it is now produced in North Yorkshire

In February 2015, Heineken (who now own the brand) announced that it was changing the recipe over fears in America that one of chemicals used for the beer's colouring could be carcinogenic. Newcastle Brown Ale is very popular in the States and one of the favourite beers of Clint Eastwood.

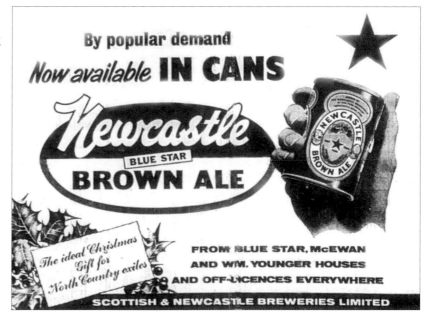

The Brown Ale Opera Singer

As part of an advertising campaign in the 1960s, Owen Brannigan sang the following lyrics to the tune of the North East classic 'Cushy Butterfield'

> *If you want a beer that's perfection indeed*
> *I give you a guide to fulfilling your need,*
> *At home by the fireside, in club or in bar*
> *The sign of good taste is the famous Blue Star*
> *It's the strong beer, it's the bottled beer*
> *With the North's biggest sale*
> *For complete satisfaction*
> *Newcastle Brown Ale.*

Annitsford-born Brannigan (*right*) was a very popular singer from the 1940s to early '70s and was known for his wide musical range – from Mozart to Gilbert & Sullivan as well as traditional North East songs. In 1960 he recorded 'Folk Songs from Northumbria' with Gerald Moore that included the original 'Cushy Butterfield', 'Dance Ti' Thee Daddy' and 'Keep Your Feet Still, Geordie Hinney'.

Amber Ale

Left: An advert for 'Newcastle Amber Ale' that was brewed until the 1980s. This was a 'lighter' ale than Newcastle Brown and was a diluted version of Exhibition.

For some, Brown Ale was too strong and so Amber Ale was developed.

James Deuchar and Lochside Ale

From humble beginnings in the 1860s, Scottish-born James Deuchar eventually owned a large number of pubs in Newcastle, Gateshead and Sunderland as well as the Lochside Brewery in Montrose. The company's Scottish ales were brought to the North East by sea on two steamers, 'Lochside' then later 'Lochside II'. James Deuchar Ltd was bought by Newcastle Breweries in 1956.

The Lochside in Red Hall Drive, Heaton was opened just before Deuchar's was taken over by Newcastle Breweries. Still open in 2015, it is one of the last surviving reminders of the James Deuchar pub and brewing empire.

An advert for James Deuchar's Lochside Export – 'A Better Bottled Beer' – from 1951.

The Ford Arms, Wilfred Street, Byker with an advert for Lochside Ales that can just be seen over the door on the right.

Robert Deuchar and Duddingston Ales

Right: The former Sandyford Brewery of Robert Deuchar. He started brewing at Sandyford in the late 19th century and quickly built up a portfolio of public houses. Also around this time he bought the Duddingston Brewery outside of Edinburgh and a number of Robert Deuchar's pubs advertised their 'celebrated ales'.

Robert Deuchar's name is still above one of the doors of his old Sandyford Brewery. *Below*: Four of Robert Deuchar's Newcastle pubs.

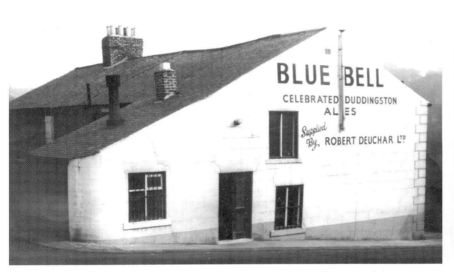

The Blue Bell, Jesmond Vale with an advert for Duddingston Ales.

The Mill Inn on Westgate Road.

The Harrogate House, Gosforth Street, Shieldfield.

The Lord Raglan Inn, Felling View, Walker. An advert for 'Celebrated Duddingston Ales' has almost worn away on the right hand wall.

Vaux and Double Maxim

Today, a number of 'soft drinks' are advertised for their energy giving powers but 80 years ago this 'man's drink' was promoted for its 'health giving properties'. Maxim Ale was first brewed in 1901 and named after the Maxim Gun Attachment that was commanded by Major Ernest Vaux of the Sunderland brewing family. The ale's strength was increased in 1938 and it was renamed Double Maxim.

The Vaux family started brewing in Sunderland in the 1830s. The company built a major brewery in the centre of the town and acquired pubs throughout the North East. There were a number of Vaux pubs in Newcastle, including the Kenton Bar Inn (*right*), the Percy Arms (page 12), the Tanners Arms (page 13), the Windmill Inn (page 37) and the two pubs below.

The Vaux Brewery was closed in 1999, however, former directors formed the Double Maxim Beer Company to carry on brewing former brands. Now based in Houghton-le-Spring, the company produces traditional beers such as Samson, Ward's Best Bitter and of course its namesake – Double Maxim.

The Rose & Crown, Walker Road.

The Half Moon Hotel, Byker.

James Robinson & Sons

Right: The barrels of wine and spirit merchants, James Robinson & Sons. The company, founded in 1827, was based in the Cloth Market for many years and survived until the area was redeveloped in the 1970s. A 1911 advert for Strathvegan Finest Old Scotch Whiskey supplied by Robinson's was described as being 'recommended by the medical profession' with a quote from the *London Medical Record*: 'An article that may be relied on, which may be safely recommended by the physician. It has the true flavour of well-matured whiskey, and is mellow and delicate to the palate.'

A delivery of Harp Lager to the Three Mile Inn on the Great North Road, Gosforth.

Harp

Lager started to become popular in local pubs in the 1960s and Harp was one of a number of brands introduced at that time. It was originally brewed by Guinness then a number of companies, including Scottish & Newcastle, joined forces to produce the lager.

Harp is still brewed by Diageo – the name Guinness have traded under since a merger in 1997.

The Price of Beer

In the 1970s, Harp and other local beers doubled in price over five years. The mid 1970s was a time of high inflation in Britain that reached over 20% at one point. Prices were rising and the cost of a pint went up as well – much to the dismay of drinkers. Here are the price rises for a pint over a five-year period.

	Price in 1972	Price in 1977
McEwan's Best Scotch	12p	$26^{1}/_{2}$p
Newcastle Exhibition	14p	28p
Harp Lager	16p	$31^{1}/_{2}$p

Prices continued to rise during the decade and, by the early 1980s, the average price of a pint was 50 pence.

Grand Hotels

Right: An artist's impression of the New Station Hotel, Neville Street in 1889. This was an extension to the original Central Station Hotel, opened in 1850 at the same time as the adjacent station. It is now called the Royal Station Hotel.

An article in the *Newcastle Courant* of 9th March 1888 describes an attempted theft at the hotel:

'At the Newcastle Police Court yesterday, Thomas Hutton (46) was charged with attempting to steal 10s, by means of trick, from the Blackett Street Post Office … He was further charged with attempting to steal 10s, by means of a trick, from the Central Railway Station Hotel.

'Elizabeth Carnegie, clerk at the Post Office, said the prisoner came in and asked for six penny stamps. Witness supplied prisoner with the stamps, and he tendered in payment half a sovereign. Which prisoner received 9s 6d the change, he appeared to be astonished. He asked for the half sovereign back again and, putting 10s in silver beside it, requested witness to give him a sovereign for the change. Witness gave prisoner the sovereign, and he immediately left the office. In the second case Eleanor Crosthwaite barmaid at the Station Hotel said that the prisoner came into the bar with another man and asked for two gills of beer, for which he paid with half a sovereign. Witness gave prisoner 9s 8d change. He appeared to be very much surprised, and said he had made a mistake. He asked to have his half sovereign and having got it, he attempted to mislead the witness. Witness picked up her money and said what was called ringing the charge. She told the boots at the hotel, and the prisoner was taken into custody. The witness said she suspected the prisoner when he entered the bar. She had been 'done' by the same trick a few weeks ago. Prisoner pleaded guilty of both charges and was sent to gaol for three months on each charge.'

The old and new Gosforth Park Hotel. On the left is the Marriott Hotel Gosforth Park, shown here in 2014, that was opened in 1965 on a site near to the racecourse. On the right is the old Gosforth Park Hotel from an early 20th century postcard. In the 1880s the race course at Gosforth Park was developed and part of an old house on the estate was converted into the public house seen here. It was later renamed the Border Minstrel after a winner of the Northumberland Plate in 1927 – the most prestigious race in the North East and famously known as the Pitmen's Derby.

A postcard view of Grey Street in the mid 1950s with the Royal Turks Head Hotel on the left. The original postcard was sent to Salerno in Italy in 1955. The hotel closed in the 1980s.

It is believed that John Lennon and Paul McCartney wrote their classic song 'Love Me Do' in the Royal Turks Head in 1963. The Beatles were in Newcastle at the time during a tour with Roy Orbison and Gerry & The Pacemakers. In 2003 there were plans to place a plaque on the building to commemorate the writing of the song. However, Paul McCartney could not remember if they had stayed at the hotel or one in Jesmond and the plans for the plaque were dropped. In the 1960s bands like the Beatles were constantly touring so it would be difficult to remember a particular hotel fifty years later even if they had created a classic song there.

Above: The Royal Turks Head in the 1970s. At this time the hotel was selling Exhibition for 17 pence in the Collingwood Room, 18 pence in the Red Room and 20 pence in the Variety Room.

Left: The County Hotel, Neville Street around 1900. The hotel had been enlarged a few years before this photograph was taken. The Grade II listed building is now a Thistle Hotel with over 100 rooms.

Shields Road
Come East – Pay Least!

Shields Road in Byker is still popular for shopping and drinking and has not suffered the decline of areas in the west such as Benwell, Elswick and Scotswood. Its heyday was in the years before and after the Second World War when it had the two department stores – Parrish's and Beavan's. People would travel from throughout Tyneside, Northumberland and Durham to shop on Shields Road and no wonder when one advertising slogan from the 1950s boasted: 'Come East – Pay Least'. Today, the shops are not so busy but many of the area's pubs have survived the recent downturn in trade.

Three pubs on Shields Road that are still open today – The Raby Hotel (*above*), the Grace Inn (*left*) and the Heaton Hotel (*below*).

Above: The Heaton Hotel in 1963. Other pubs still on Shields Road are the Butchers Arms, Jacksons, and the High Main that only opened in 2013.

Right: A postcard of Shields Road with the Blue Bell in the distance. A horse and cart makes its way towards the pub. Is the barrel on the back a delivery for the Blue Bell or is it for one of the many shops in the area? Another barrel sits by the side of the road as groups of men huddle together discussing the business of the day. A tram is alongside the houses past the pub. The houses have now gone and trams replaced by the many buses that use this busy road.

Right: A close-up view of the Blue Bell from the 1960s. Behind the pub is the Odeon Cinema. The area was well served with entertainment as there was also the Apollo Cinema on Shields Road, the Grand Theatre in Wilfred Street and the Heaton Electric Palace – all now gone. Although the Palace is now a Bingo Hall.

The Blue Bell was one of the few old pubs on Shields Road to close and served its last drinks in the 1990s. Thankfully, this distinctive building was not demolished and the premises is now home to the Edinburgh Bicycle Co-operative.

Left: The Lord Clyde Hotel in the 1960s, with the Ringtons Tea factory in Algernon Road behind. Ringtons are now based in Longbenton and their old premises occupied by the auctioneers Thomas N. Miller. However, the famous tea company still use a building nearby. The Lord Clyde is still open on Shields Road in 2015.

More Pub Tales

The Crooked Billet

The Crooked Billet, seen here in 1979, survived the redevelopment of Scotswood Road in the 1960s and '70s but eventually suffered the same fate as the other pubs and closed in the '90s.

The pub's unusual name was often a topic of conversation amongst its customers. An article in the *Journal* on 26th February 1916 gave a possible explanation of its origin:

'Mr F.E. Forster applied for renewal of the licence of the Crooked Billet Scotswood Road. He stated that the chairman's question at the Brewster Sessions with regard to the origin of the name had excited a certain amount of interest, so far as the public were concerned, and several letters had been published in the press purporting to give the history of the inn. One correspondent had suggested that the origin was in connection with the billeting of soldiers by Cromwell when he was on his march from Hexham south from Newcastle. The chairman intervening said he did not think that could have any application to the name. Mr Forster then referred to another origin of the name, which was probably more applicable, and he mentioned that a correspondent of Sunderland had been kind enough to send him a copy of the *Hotel Review*. There it spoke of a 'Crooked Billet' in Beckingham Road, Penge, London, and said that the house was modern but the bowling green and skittle alley existed as in earlier times. The sign of the 'Crooked Billet' was a ragged staff which was cut from a large tree outside the original wayside inn, when the whole district round about did not contain any other habitation. It had been said that the 'Crooked Billet' in this district might correspond to a piece of iron which did not mould itself, when put under the hammer to the desired form. This was only another speculation as to the origins of the name. Mr Forster concluded by proving that the recent conduct of the house had not been sufficiently crooked to warrant the bench in refusing its licence. The licence was granted.'

The George & Dragon

Left: Inside the George & Dragon, Eldon Square, with a selection of the food on offer in the 1970s. The menu in this Scottish & Newcastle pub had a strong North of the Border flavour:

Caeriave Stew (braised steak and vegetables) for 70 pence.

Alloway Bridie (minced beef, ham and bacon cooked in pastry) for 55 pence.

Cup-a-soup – Brawd Bree (hare and rabbit broth) for 14 pence.

The Balloon Goes Up

The Balloon (*right*) was built on
Silver Lonnen, Fenham, in the 1950s
and named after a barrage balloon
stationed in the area during the
Second World War. The building
survived less than ten years and was
replaced with a more permanent
structure, also called the Balloon,
that still stands today (*below right*).

A barrage balloon like this one was
based at Silver Lonnen as one of the
defences against the Luftwaffe.

The Windmill Comes Down

Today Cowgate is a very
built-up area with
housing estates,
supermarkets and busy
roads. However, the
postcard on the left from
a hundred years ago
shows a much more rural
scene. The Windmill is
shown in a state of
disrepair but the Mill Inn
was thriving at the time.
In the early 1900s John
Smart was the licensee
and at the far left of the
pub a board can just be
seen with his name on it.

Houses started being
built in Cowgate in the
years between the two
world wars and, by the
1930s, the Mill Inn (and
the windmill) were
pulled down to make way
for the Windmill Inn seen
here on the left.

There was further
redevelopment in
Cowgate in the 1990s and
this former Vaux pub was
demolished.

The Green Tree

The Green Tree, Old Benwell, N C on Tyne.   (123)

Above: A picture postcard of 'The Green Tree, Old Benwell' in the early 1900s. The Hawthorn Inn is next door. At this time, Benwell looked like the peaceful village scene we see here. The area was soon to change with dozens of streets being built and the Green Tree was too small to meet the needs of the growing population. In the 1930s it was redeveloped and extended (*left*). The pub continued to serve the people of Benwell for a further sixty years before being demolished.

In its final few years, local boxer John Davison ran 'boxercise' classes at the Green Tree. John, a former WBC International Featherweight champion, combined a fitness class with the skills of boxing.

Right: John Davison with the WBC International Featherweight belt he won in 1990.

Left: The Green Tree Inn, Benwell in the 1960s.

Sporting Connections – Boxing

Boxing, like football, has a number of connections with pubs in Newcastle.

In the 1920s the Forth Hotel in Pink Lane (*right*) was owned by former world heavyweight boxing champion Tommy Burns (*below*). Burns was born in Canada in 1881

and, despite being only 5 ft 7 ins tall, won the heavyweight crown in 1906. He then travelled the world, defending his title on eleven occasions. One fight was against Benwell-born Jack Palmer who Tommy knocked out after four rounds. He finally lost the title to American Jack Johnson.

Another boxer who became a Newcastle publican was Will Curley. On 2nd November 1899 he fought Canadian George Dixon for the world featherweight title in New York. Dixon was declared the winner on points after 25 rounds. The crowd felt Curley had won and threw cushions in the ring when the decision was announced.

Curley used the money he had earned in the ring to invest in pubs on Tyneside – the Crown & Sceptre in High Friar Street, Newcastle and the Phoenix on Gateshead High Street. They were popular with locals who gave both pubs the nickname 'Curley's'.

Curley stayed in the pub trade for over 50 years as well as being an investor in St James' Hall in Newcastle which became the top boxing venue in the city.

Will Curley – Tyneside boxer and publican.

Customers gathered outside Will Curley's Newcastle pub, the Crown & Sceptre in High Friar Street. The pub closed its doors for the final time in the early 1970s.

All Change in the 1960s and '70s

The 1960s and '70s saw a radical change in architecture in Britain – and pubs were no exception. Newcastle embraced this new age and its biggest champion was council leader T. Dan Smith. Traditional streets and buildings were seen as old fashioned and were torn down to be replaced by new roads, high rise flats, shops and office blocks. Breweries built a number of pubs around these new developments and several had the distinctive flat roofs that were so popular at the time. Architects boasted of their radical designs but many of these new buildings had structural flaws and were disliked by the public. Some of the pubs that were built at this time have already been demolished.

Right: The Man on the Moon in Princess Square opened in the early 1970s with its name coming from the new 'space age'. In 1969 Neil Armstrong had become the first man to walk on the moon. The pub had rooms that were named the 'Launch Pad' and the 'Crater Bar'. The pub is still open today and now called Trillians.

One of the first of these new pubs was the Printers Pie, Pudding Chare which was opened in the early '60s. Situated behind the Chronicle building, it is now called Fleet Street and in 2015 is up for lease.

The Turbinia, Fossway, Walker was opened in the late '60s. Although a modern pub, it has a traditional name. The Tyneside-built 'Turbinia' was the world's first steam turbine-driven vessel in 1897.

Two pubs built in the '70s as part of shopping developments that are no longer with us. The Whin Dyke at Denton Park (*above left*) and the Adelaide, Benwell (*above right*).

Inside and outside of the Nelson, Church Walk, Walker, just after opening in 1970. The interior fixtures included a television set – unusual at the time but now seen in almost every pub.

Right: A Chieftain tank arrives in Cruddas Park on 1st December 1969 for the opening of a pub named in its honour. The Chieftain pub took its name from the tank built at the nearby Vickers Factory on Scotswood Road. An advert produced for the pub's opening night gave this description of its 'themed' interior:

'The military emphasis is immediately apparent on entry with skilful use of a photo mural placed opposite the main door. It shows a tank run by the 15th/19th the King's Royal Hussars and the driver, a local boy, adds some extra Geordie flavour to the surroundings.

'The bar for instance, is a long alcove room with a floor-covered by a patterned linoleum whose design strongly resembles a tank track imprint. Narrow width pine panelling in the walls sharply contrasts with the smooth cherry veneer used elsewhere. A photo mural in the bar, depicting a cut through interior of the Chieftain tank, is used as a wall decoration opposite the counter. And to enhance further what can be safely described as a unique décor is the counter front which is decorated with solid black pads on a sandy background, reminiscent of the inset rubber pads used in the tank's caterpillar tracks.

'The lounge for a combination of eye appeal and ingenuity takes some beating. Entering through a short curved passage there is a scaled down low relief representation of the lower portion of the Chieftain tank namely tank track and road wheels. This is a fibre glass reproduction mounted to the counter front (*left*). On the left of this tank is a small armoury of shells. Possibly the pub's principal feature, although it will be considered by many that every aspect is a special feature, is a 120 mm gun, seen in profile, starkly silhouetted against a brightly lit camouflaged background, forming the back fitment to the lounge bar.'

New Life for Old Pubs

Many of the pubs featured in this book have been closed and in most cases demolished. It is sad to see a popular pub that was a part of the local community disappear, however, on these pages we see former pubs whose buildings have been given a new lease of life. Although they may not be their old selves, the buildings have been preserved and serve the community in a different way.

The Hawthorn Inn on Forth Banks is now an Indian restaurant.

The Grapes on Grey Street in the 1960s. Within two decades this city centre pub was closed. Today it is now part of HSBC Bank and looking at the photograph below you would think the pub had never existed. The two ornate lamp-posts have hardly changed in fifty years.

Another restaurant in 2015 is the former Sporting Arms on Denton Road.

The Bay Horse on Westgate Road is now a shop selling leather wear in 2015.

The King Arms on the corner of Diana Street and Douglas Terrace, Arthur's Hill. The photograph below shows the old pub today, painted white and converted for residential and business use. However, not all trace of its old life has disappeared. Under the paint can just be seen the old name 'The Kings Arms' (below).

Temperance

The Temperance movement, where people abstained from alcohol, was very popular from the 1830s till the mid 20th century. Newcastle was no exception from this worldwide campaign and there were a number of hotels that did not serve alcohol to cater for the non-drinking traveller. Kelly's Trade Directory of 1929 listed the following Temperance Hotels:

Cassidy, Miss Francis, 104 Newgate Street

Clyde, Miss N. Cleverly, 18 Westmorland Road

Empire Temperance Hotel, 1 Nun's Lane

Hume, Miss Jane, 18 Wentworth Place

Livingstone, J., 52 Newgate Street

Portland Commercial, 21 Portland Terrace

Punton, Mrs E., 14 Bath Lane

Queen's Hotel, 37 Westmorland Road

Tyne Temperance Hotel, 13 Hood Street

Whinship's Hotel, 75 Clayton Street

There were further hotels in Alnwick, Berwick, Morpeth, Wallsend and Whitley Bay.

Two photographs of the former Temperance Hotel, the Clarendon, Clayton Street. The image above is from a postcard produced by the hotel and sent to Windermere by a guest in 1915. The photo below was taken a hundred years later. Today, Clarendon House contains shops, a restaurant and apartments.

CADET FORWARD MOVEMENT

The tall chrysanth, so fair and sweet,

With scent and beauty loves to greet;

So may Cadets, both girls and boys,

In *service* find their truest joys.

Left: A Cadets of Temperance postcard. This was one of several groups which targeted children when warning of the problems associated with drinking. One of the most popular groups was the Band of Hope, who, in 1881, published a Hymn Book that sold nearly three million copies. Members of groups such as these were encouraged to 'sign the pledge' which promised they would refrain from alcohol.

In Newcastle, the Heaton Anti-licensing Council was very active in opposing licences for new public houses. Only two pubs were built in Heaton in the late 19th and early 20th centuries – the Chillingham Hotel and the Corner House. This heavily-populated suburb with so few pubs was said to be a 'dry' area.

Last Orders

We end with some final images of pubs, their customers and special days to remember.

Above: Another photograph of a charabanc outing, this time a group of women leave from the George the First, George Street, Elswick in the 1920s.

Right: The original Cradle Well, Jesmond Road, before it was rebuilt in the early 1900s. Above the door is the name 'John Espie Wine & Spirit Merchant. The second Cradlewell can be seen on page 16.

Below: The Bobby Shaftoe on the corner of Armstrong Road and Ranmere Road, Scotswood. Crowds flocked to see the opening of the new pub in the early 1960s (*below right*).

In December 1955 an unusual opening for a pub took place at the Northumberland Hussar on Sackville Road, Heaton (*right*). Men from the regiment played a trumpet fanfare while their commanding officer Lieutenant Colonel N.H.R. Speke performed the opening ceremony. The Northumberland Hussar was one of four pubs that Newcastle Breweries opened that month. The others being the Red House in Blyth, the Centurion in Throckley and the Northumberland Fusilier in Forest Hall.

A trumpet fanfare at the opening of the Northumberland Hussar.

The Hussars enjoy a pint in the pub named after their regiment on opening night in 1955.

Above: An upstairs room in the Northumberland Arms with bells on the tables for customers to ring for service.

Left: Bourgognes on Newgate Street in the late 1960s. In the following decade it was one of several pubs knocked down for the Eldon Square Shopping Centre. An advert on the pub for Younger Ales claims: 'Get Younger Every Day'.

Above: Outside the Pine Apple Inn, Elswick, on Sunday, 24th May 1914, this group (including the local vicar) are ready to go on a trip to Wooler. Although, it is likely that this was a 'men only trip' and the children in the photo (and possibly the vicar) were only posing for the photographer before seeing the men off.

Right: Inside and outside the Hydraulic Crane, Scotswood Road, in the early 1960s. The top photograph shows the pub's tables and chairs outside while customers wait for the centenary procession of the Blaydon Races in 1962. Today, seeing drinkers outside a pub is common but fifty years ago it was only for special occasions. The bottom photo shows plenty of happy faces on both sides of the bar.

Bibliography and Further Reading

Brewers & Bottlers of Newcastle upon Tyne by Brian Bennison
(Newcastle City Library and Arts 1995)

Heady Days – A History of Newcastle's Public Houses: Volume One the Central Area
by Brian Bennison (Newcastle City Library and Arts 1996)

Heavy Nights – A History of Newcastle's Public Houses: Volume Two the North and East
by Brian Bennison (Newcastle City Library and Arts 1997)

Lost Weekends – A History of Newcastle's Public Houses: Volume Three the West
by Brian Bennison (Newcastle City Library and Arts 1998)

The Old Pubs of Gateshead by John Boothroyd (Summerhill Books 2014)

Westenders – Memories of Arthur's Hill, Benwell, Elswick & Scotswood by Yvonne Young
(Summerhill Books 2010)

North East Boxing Book by Alan Brett & Billy Wood (Black Cat Publications 1995)

Allan's Tyneside Songs (1891)

Kelly's and Ward's Trade Directories

Newspapers and Periodicals

Newcastle Journal   *Evening Chronicle*

Newcastle Courant   *Sunderland Echo*

Monthly Chronicle of North Country Lore and Legend (1888)

An advert for W.B. Reid, Brewers and Wine &
Spirit Merchants, who operated for over 100
years from the 1830s. The advert shows their
Grey Street premises and Leazes Brewery.

Index of Pubs & Hotels

Also available from Summerhill Books

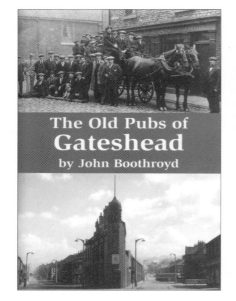

The Old Pubs of Gateshead
by John Boothroyd

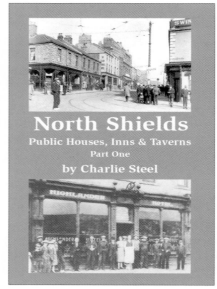

North Shields
Public Houses, Inns & Taverns
Part One
by Charlie Steel

North Shields
Public Houses, Inns & Taverns
Part Two
by Charlie Steel
Including Tynemouth, Cullercoats, Whitley Bay and District

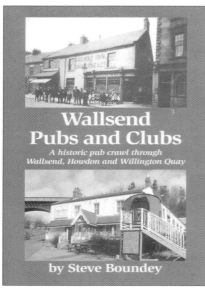

Wallsend Pubs and Clubs
A historic pub crawl through
Wallsend, Howdon and Willington Quay
by Steve Boundey

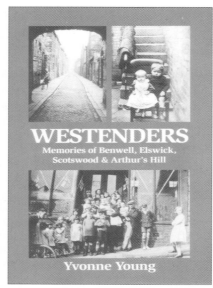

WESTENDERS
Memories of Benwell, Elswick, Scotswood & Arthur's Hill
Yvonne Young

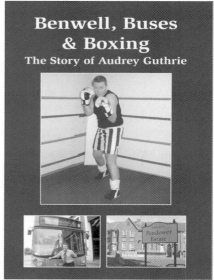

Benwell, Buses & Boxing
The Story of Audrey Guthrie

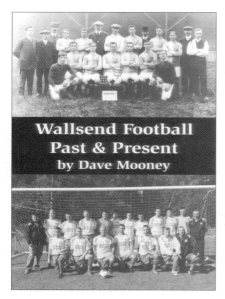

Wallsend Football Past & Present
by Dave Mooney

Deaths, Disasters & Dastardly Deeds
in the North East
by Lorna Windham

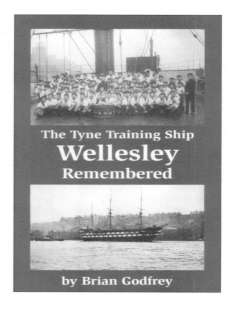

The Tyne Training Ship Wellesley Remembered
by Brian Godfrey

www.summerhillbooks.co.uk